8/24

Read for a Better World ™

RAINY DAYS
A First Look

PERCY LEED

Lerner Publications ◆ Minneapolis

Educator Toolbox

Reading books is a great way for kids to express what they're interested in. Before reading this title, ask the reader these questions:

What do you think this book is about? Look at the cover for clues.

What do you already know about rainy days?

What do you want to learn about rainy days?

Let's Read Together

Encourage the reader to use the pictures to understand the text.

Point out when the reader successfully sounds out a word.

Praise the reader for recognizing sight words such as *is* and *it*.

TABLE OF CONTENTS

Rainy Days

It is a rainy day!
The rain is wet.

When it is rainy,
the sky is gray.

A rainy day is gloomy.

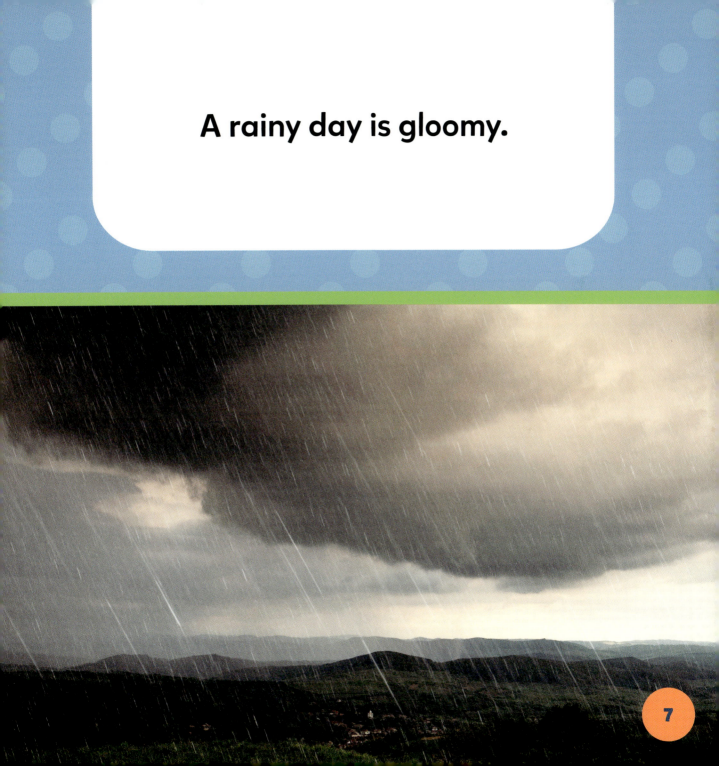

When it is rainy,
clouds fill the sky.
Rain falls from
the clouds.

What else falls from clouds?

When it is rainy,
flowers grow.
We see a rainbow.

When it is rainy,
it can flood.

What else can happen in a rainstorm?

Lightning can strike.

When it is rainy,
rabbits hide.

Ducks swim in the rain.

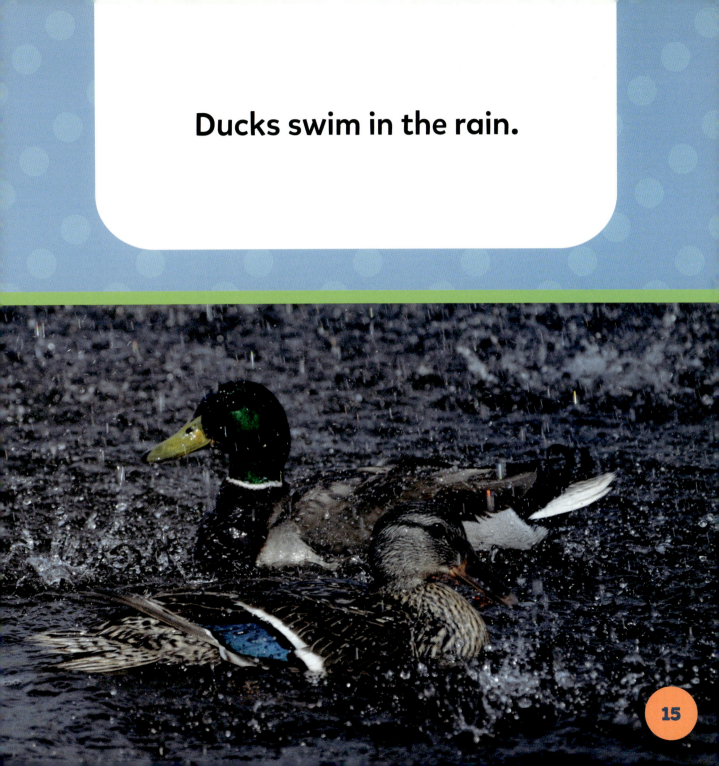

When it is rainy,
we put on
a raincoat.
We open
an umbrella.

What do you
wear when it rains?

When it is rainy,
we can splash.

A rainy day is fun!

You Connect!

What is something you like about rainy days?

What have you noticed animals do in the rain?

What do you like to do on a rainy day?

STEM Snapshot

Encourage students to think and ask questions like a scientist! Ask the reader:

What is something you learned about rainy days?

What is something you noticed about rainy days in the pictures in this book?

What is something you still don't know about rainy days?

Photo Glossary

flood

lightning

rainbow

umbrella

Learn More

Carlson-Berne, Emma. *Let's Explore the Water Cycle*. Minneapolis: Lerner Publications, 2021.

DK Publishing. *Weather and the Seasons*. New York: DK Publishing, 2019.

Peters, Katie. *Look at the Rain*. Minneapolis: Lerner Publications, 2020.

Index

clouds, 8, 9
ducks, 15

flood, 12
flowers, 11
lightning, 13

rabbits, 14
raincoat, 16

Photo Acknowledgments

The images in this book are used with the permission of: © KAMONRAT/Shutterstock Images, pp. 4–5, 23; © Tetiana Soares/Adobe Stock, p. 6; © andreiuc88/Adobe Stock, p. 7; © SusanneSchulz/iStockphoto, pp. 8–9; © KAY4YK/Shutterstock Images, pp. 10–11, 23; © William Lee/Adobe Stock, p. 11; © Eugene Feygin/Adobe Stock, pp. 12, 23; © bgfoto/iStockphoto, pp. 13, 23; © stanley45/iStockphoto, p. 14; © Landscapes, nature, macro/iStockphoto, p. 15; © torwai/iStockphoto, pp. 16–17; © amriphoto/iStockphoto, pp. 18–19; © PeopleImages.com - Yuri A/Shutterstock Images, p. 20.

Cover Photograph: © Kirsten Davis/peopleimages.com/Adobe Stock

Design Elements: © Mighty Media, Inc.

Copyright © 2024 by Lerner Publishing Group, Inc.

Lerner Publications Company
An imprint of Lerner Publishing Group, Inc.
241 First Avenue North
Minneapolis, MN 55401 USA

For reading levels and more information, look up this title at www.lernerbooks.com.

Main body text set in Mikado a Medium.
Typeface provided by Hannes von Doehren.

Library of Congress Cataloging-in-Publication Data

Names: Leed, Percy, 1968–author.
Title: Rainy days : a first look / Percy Leed.
Description: Minneapolis : Lerner Publications, [2024] | Series: Read about weather (read for a better world) | Includes bibliographical references and index. | Audience: Ages 5–8 | Audience: Grades K–1 | Summary: "Rainy days can be dark and gloomy, but they can also be fun and colorful! Engaging photographs and leveled text encourage young readers to enjoy learning more about rainy days"—Provided by publisher.
Identifiers: LCCN 2023006945 (print) | LCCN 2023006946 (ebook) | ISBN 9798765608784 (library binding) | ISBN 9798765616741 (epub)
Subjects: LCSH: Rain and rainfall—Juvenile literature. | Weather—Juvenile literature. | BISAC: JUVENILE NONFICTION / Science & Nature / Earth Sciences / Weather
Classification: LCC QC924.7 .L45 2024 (print) | LCC QC924.7 (ebook) | DDC 551.57/7—dc23/eng20230714

LC record available at https://lccn.loc.gov/2023006945
LC ebook record available at https://lccn.loc.gov/2023006946

Manufactured in the United States of America
1 – CG – 12/15/23

24